Building Stories

Isabel Hill

Star Bright Books
New York

To my daughter, Anna, who continues to show me how to see things differently.

—I.H.

Published in the United States of America by Star Bright Books, Inc., 30-19 48th Avenue, Long Island City, NY 11101.

The name Star Bright Books and the Star Bright Books logo are registered trademarks of Star Bright Books, Inc. Please visit www.starbrightbooks.com.

For bulk orders, contact: orders@starbrightbooks.com, or call customer service at: (718) 784-9112.

Hardback ISBN-13: 978-1-59572-279-9
Paperback ISBN-13: 978-1-59572-280-5

Star Bright Books / NY / 00103110

Library of Congress Cataloging-in-Publication Data

Hill, Isabel (Isabel T.)
 Building stories / by Isabel Hill.
    p. cm.
 Summary: Rhyming text and photographs of icons on buildings invite the reader to guess what was done or made in each building originally. Includes "stories characters and plots" of the buildings, as well as their settings.
  ISBN 978-1-59572-279-9 (hardback) -- ISBN 978-1-59572-280-5 (pbk.)
  [1. Stories in rhyme. 2. Buildings--Fiction.] I. Title.
  PZ8.3.H55112Bui 2011
  [E]--dc22
                              2010050860

Buildings are like books with stories that last.
They tell us about our present and also our past.

The outside of a building says quite a lot,
About setting, about character, and even about plot.

Think of the setting as a building's address
Or its date of construction, so you don't have to guess.

Look for the characters in each storyline,
People or animals in the building's design.

For plot, it's what happened or what was made there,
The action, the conflict, the reason we care.

Yellow pencils standing on an industrial place,

Illustrate what was manufactured in this space.

5

This nurse, a main character, a caretaking force,

On the face of what building? A hospital, of course.

7

A triangle, a bell, a violin, a drum,

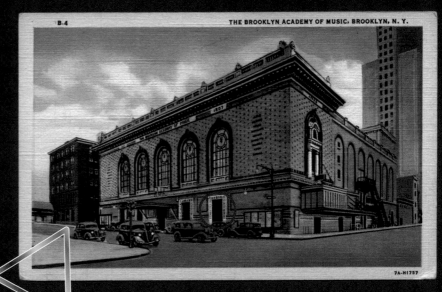

THE BROOKLYN ACADEMY OF MUSIC, BROOKLYN, N. Y.

A melodic theme makes this music hall hum.

9

Oars steer this ship as it navigates its way,

On a YMCA where only sailors could stay.

11

This movie theater was hopping when it was brand new.

A mother, a daughter, a boy with his hound,

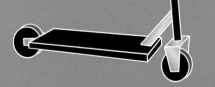

In this apartment complex as big as a town.

15

Valves, pipes and hydrants—the stage has been set.

For a drama about firefighters and the challenges they met.

The dime on this building was a symbolic detail,

For an important savings bank of monumental scale.

Can you figure out the plot when you see each cool cow?

Milk was bottled in this plant and we can see how!

This old-fangled telephone was a new way to speak,

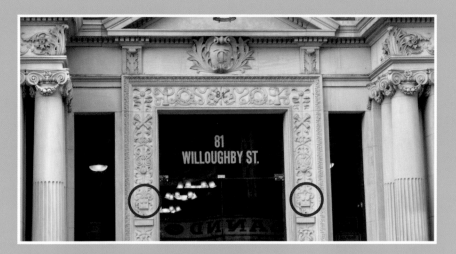

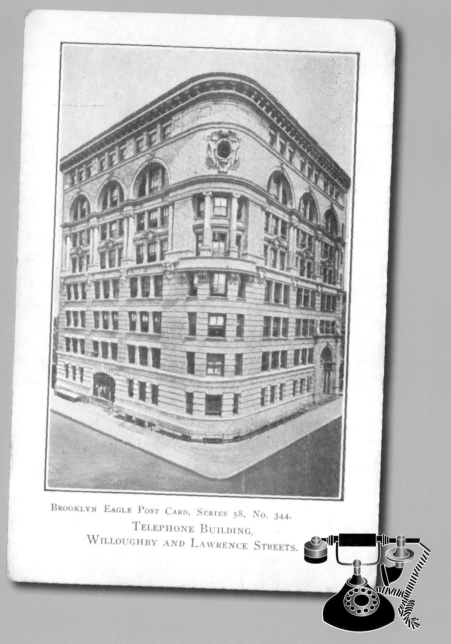

BROOKLYN EAGLE POST CARD, SERIES 58, No. 344.
TELEPHONE BUILDING,
WILLOUGHBY AND LAWRENCE STREETS.

Those who worked in this office brought us something unique.

A student is a character with a book as his tool,

Fourth Avenue and 13th Street is the site for this school.

Lions, monkeys, and elephants to name just a few,

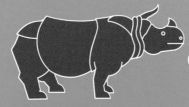

Of the characters on these buildings at a famous zoo.

27

What was the story behind these bundles of wheat?

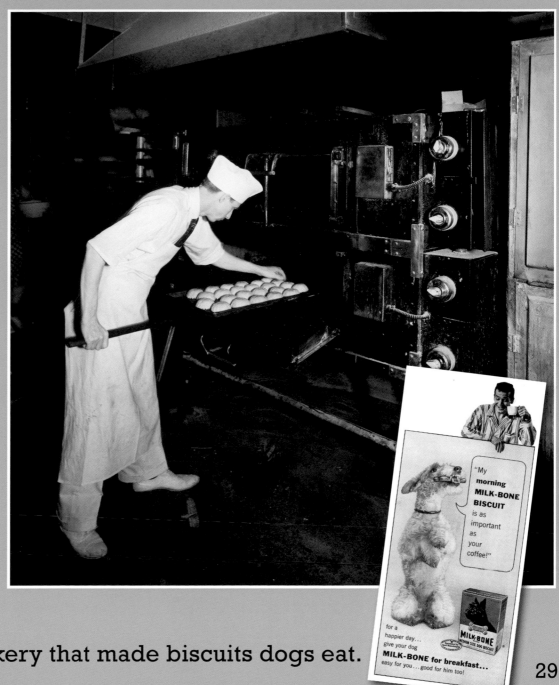

This was a bakery that made biscuits dogs eat.

Playing tennis and baseball at an indoor location?

Yes, inside this gym there are all kinds of recreation.

A big wheel with wings, what a magical sight!

On a garage where your car can spend the whole night.

33

You've uncovered the plots and know what these buildings are about,

And the characters and settings help to spell it all out.

Reading a building is exciting and fun,

So start at the beginning and don't stop 'til you're done.

Characters and Plots

(Page 4) Eberhard Faber Pencil Company Building—The Eberhard Faber Pencil Company was one of Brooklyn's most important manufacturers. On the outside of the building are giant yellow pencils sharpened to a perfect point. They are just like the ones that were made inside this factory, which employed mostly women.

(Page 6) Student Nurses' Residence, St. Vincent's Hospital—St. Vincent's Hospital began as a 30-bed hospital to take care of poor and disadvantaged New Yorkers. The nurse on the outside shows us that this particular building was used as the nurses' residence while they were being taught how to take care of patients in St. Vincent's Hospital.

(Page 8) Brooklyn Academy of Music—The Brooklyn Academy of Music is still a popular performing arts center, with three separate spaces for music and theater. Details of musical instruments around the entrances along with the names of famous musicians cut into the brick façade illustrate the overall musical theme.

(Page 10) Naval Branch/YMCA Building—When completed, the Naval Branch of the YMCA had 200 rooms for sleeping and also a 500-seat auditorium, a swimming pool, bowling alleys, a library, and several restaurants. Boats on each corner of the building show that this was a special home for sailors when they came ashore.

(Page 12) Claremont Theater—The Claremont Theater is one of New York City's oldest structures built specifically to show movies or motion pictures, as they were originally called. On the front, you will find an early movie camera resting on a stand or tripod.

(Page 14) Parkchester Apartments—When Parkchester was completed, it had 12,273 apartments. It was very much like a small town with stores, a movie theater, a bowling alley, and several beautiful parks. On many of the buildings there are decorations that show the lives of ordinary people, like you and me, who lived at Parkchester.

(Page 16) Department of Water Supply, Gas, and Electricity Building— In this building, repairs were made to special fire hydrants, like the one you see in the picture. These hydrants provided more water than the regular ones and were needed in places where the buildings were bigger or where there were more buildings concentrated in a neighborhood.

(Page 18) Dime Savings Bank of Brooklyn—The Dime Savings Bank was the largest savings institution in Brooklyn. The building was built to look like an ancient temple, a place of strength, power and wealth. Would you have guessed from seeing the dime on the outside, that you only needed a dime to open an account?

(Page 20) Empire State Dairy/Borden's Milk Plant—The Empire State Dairy, later named Borden's Milk Plant, was a place of production and distribution. Raw cows' milk arrived here and was made into processed milk, and other dairy products. The cows on the exterior are set in a pastoral scene, a contrast to the busy Brooklyn street where the plant is located.

(Page 22) New York & New Jersey Telephone Company Building—The New York & New Jersey Telephone Company had its offices in this building. Inside, there were large switchboards where operators connected the telephone calls. Over 16,000 calls were connected in the building's first year. The odd-looking telephone over the entrance gives us an idea of what telephones used to look like.

(Page 24) Public School 124—Around the beginning of the 1900s, the population of New York City was rapidly expanding. Many new school buildings, such as Public School 124, were built for immigrants coming from all over the world. The open book on the front of this building identifies it as a place where learning and knowledge are available to everyone.

(Page 26) The New York Zoological Park/Bronx Zoo—The New York Zoological Society/Bronx Zoo was built to teach people about animals and their natural habitats. When it was first constructed, the zoo had 20,000 visitors a day. Specific buildings with elaborate animal sculptures were built to house different species of monkeys, elephants and lions.

(Page 28) Wheatsworth Bakery Building—Wheatsworth Bakery was a large manufacturer of whole wheat biscuits and flour. Right inside this building, the first Milk Bone Dog Biscuit was made! The building operated as a bakery until the mid-1950s and the bundles of wheat are still a reminder of what went into making these biscuits.

(Page 30) West Side YMCA Building—With its elaborate terra-cotta entrances, the West Side YMCA looks like an old palace. It was built to provide housing and recreational/social activities for young men. Different sports that took place inside are shown on the outside entrances of the building.

(Page 32) S & L Corporation Car Garage—By the late 1920s, as cars became more affordable, there was a growing need for public parking. This is one of the many car garages built at that time in New York City. The tires on the S & L Corporation Car Garage are the perfect entrance to this five-story building.

Settings/Historical Photo Credits

Eberhard Faber Pencil Building
47-61 Greenpoint Avenue, Brooklyn, NY
Built: 1923-24
Architect: Frederick H. Clie
Bottom left, top right: Courtesy of the
Collection of the Brooklyn Historical Society,
Brooklyn, NY; bottom right: Courtesy of Bruce
M. Craig, Washington, DC

Student Nurses' Residence, St. Vincent's Hospital
158 West 12th Street, New York, NY
Built: 1924
Architect: I. E. Ditmars
Bottom left, right: Courtesy of the Sisters of
Charity, Bronx, NY

Brooklyn Academy of Music
30 Lafayette Avenue, Brooklyn, NY
Built: 1908
Architects: Herts & Tallant
Top right: Courtesy of the Brooklyn Public
Library—Brooklyn Collection, Brooklyn,
NY; bottom right: Courtesy of Photography
Collection, Miriam and Ira D. Wallach
Division of Art, Prints and Photographs, The
New York Public Library, Astor, Lenox and
Tilden Foundations, New York, NY

Naval Branch/YMCA Building
167 Sands Street, Brooklyn, NY
Built: 1901-1902
Architects: Parish & Schroeder
Bottom left, right: Courtesy of Kautz Family
YMCA Archives, University of Minnesota
Libraries, Minneapolis, MN

Claremont Theater
3320-3338 Broadway, New York, NY
Built: 1914
Architect: Gaetano Ajello
Bottom left: Bert Hardy, photographer/Hulton
Archive, Courtesy of Getty Images, Seattle,
WA; top right: Courtesy of the Museum of
the City of New York, Wurts Bros., Collection,
ca. 1915, New York, NY; bottom right: William
Vanderson, photographer/Hulton Archive,
Courtesy of Getty Images, Seattle, WA

Parkchester Apartments
East Tremont to McGraw Avenues, Purdy
Street to White Plains Road, Bronx, NY
Built: 1939-42
Architects: Associated Architects
Bottom left: Courtesy of The Bronx County
Historical Society, Bronx, NY; right: Alfred
Eisenstaedt, photographer/Hulton Archive,
Courtesy of Getty Images, Seattle, WA

Department of Water Supply, Gas, and Electricity Building
226 West Broadway, New York, NY
Built: 1912
Architect: Augustus D. Shepard, Jr.
Center: Department of Finance, Tax Photos,
Courtesy of NYC Municipal Archives, New
York, NY; top right: Mayor's Reception
Committee, WWI, ca. 1920s, Courtesy of NYC
Municipal Archives, New York, NY; bottom
right: NYC Fire Department, Courtesy of NYC
Municipal Archives, New York, NY

Dime Savings Bank of Brooklyn
9 DeKalb Avenue, Brooklyn, NY
Built: 1908
Architects: Mobray & Uffinger
Bottom left, top right: Courtesy of the
Brooklyn Public Library—Brooklyn
Collection, Brooklyn, NY; bottom right:
Copyright © CLM, Shutterstock Images